H. C. G. Moule

Thoughts on Christian Sanctity

H. C. G. Moule

Thoughts on Christian Sanctity

ISBN/EAN: 9783743305465

Manufactured in Europe, USA, Canada, Australia, Japa

Cover: Foto ©Lupo / pixelio.de

Manufactured and distributed by brebook publishing software (www.brebook.com)

H. C. G. Moule

Thoughts on Christian Sanctity

THOUGHTS ON
CHRISTIAN SANCTITY

Thoughts
ON
Christian Sanctity

BY

H. C. G. MOULE, M.A.

Principal of Ridley Hall, *and late Fellow of* Trinity College, Cambridge

"The God of Peace .. make you perfect in every good work to do His will . through Jesus Christ."—Heb. xiii. 20, 21.

Twenty-seventh Thousand

LONDON
Seeley & Co., Essex Street, Strand
1888

CONTENTS

I.
AIMS, LIMITS, POSSIBILITIES . . . 9   PAGE

II.
SELF-DENIAL AND THE DAILY CROSS . 21

III.
GOD IS ABLE 34

IV.
THE DIVINE MASTER 45

V.
THE DIVINE KEEPER 58

VI.
THE DIVINE FRIEND 71

VII.
CHRIST DWELLING IN THE HEART . . 83

VIII.
MOTIVES AND MEANS . . . 9?

IX.
SOME PRACTICAL INFERENCES . . . 106

X.
HYMNS 119

PREFATORY NOTE

THE following chapters, except the third and the ninth, reproduce nearly word for word a series of addresses delivered to the " Cambridge University Church Society," in the October term of 1884.

They are offered to the reader with entire submission of the contents to the authority of the Holy criptures, and with the earnest prayer that the Eternal Master will mercifully use for His work whatever in them is of His truth.

The Scripture quotations are made, as a rule, from the Authorized Version, with an occasional variation where a more literal rendering appeared to add point or force.

" How blest are they who still abide
Close shelter'd in Thy bleeding side !
Who life and strength from Thee derive,
And by Thee move, and in Thee live.

" Firstborn of many brethren Thou !
To Thee, lo, all our souls we bow ;
To Thee our hearts and hands we give;
Thine may we die, Thine may we live."

      ZINZENDORF, tr. WESLEY.

Christian Sanctity

I.

AIMS, LIMITS, POSSIBILITIES.

THE subject of these chapters needs little introduction. It has to do with the very life of the life of the individual Christian, and of the Christian Church. It is nothing less than the supreme aim of the Christian Gospel, that we should be holy; that the God of Peace should sanctify us through and through our being; that we should "walk worthy of the Lord unto all pleasing," "all studious meeting of His will," as the Greek of Col. i. 10 imports. At the blessed Table ever and again we "present ourselves, soul and body, a living sacrifice," and ask, in a spiritual attitude of entire receptivity, to " be *fulfilled* with

[margin: 1 Thess. v. 23. Col. i. 10.]

His grace and heavenly benediction." In the morning worship of our Church we pray twice over to be "kept this day without sin."

It is the insatiable desire of the soul, which has truly seen the Lord, to be made fully like Him by His grace. And this desire, as it has never been wholly absent from His congregation, has, in our own day and amidst our own surroundings, in a very marked degree, come again to be a leading and ruling thing. Everywhere, under widely different circumstances, in many and varied Christian communities, sometimes diverging into fields of error, sometimes moving steadily on lines of eternal truth, there is felt and found in our Christian world of to-day a deep, strong, and growing drift of enquiry and desire after Christian holiness. There is a conspicuous longing to know the whole will of God about it, and the whole offer and resource of His grace; the whole extent to which the divine warrant bids faith go in seeking, expecting, and accepting a divine deliverance from sinning, and a divine enablement to positive holiness of will and walk.

This blessed subject I propose to treat very simply and very practically. Never, I hope, in one solitary sentence, shall I forget the great lines of revealed truth and doctrine. But I do not intend to deal much with technical distinctions and definitions. I reverently accept, with deep personal conviction, at least all that our Church has defined on Original Sin. I bow to the mystery, to the fact, of the abiding " infection of nature " (Art. ix.) in the new born, and so the utter impossibility that their holiest works should " endure the severity of the divine *judgment*" (Art. xii.). But I shall touch very little upon problems of the flesh and the spirit, and the mysteries of the will. These things are immensely important in their place; but that is not, if I judge rightly, here. My present aim is to bring up in the simplest manner the remembrance of the Lord's promises, and of Himself, for actual blissful use and experience in the actings of that Life which, beyond all doubt, His people have in Him.

Our first special topic is AIMS, LIMITS, POSSIBILITIES. Let us think of each in turn.

I. AIMS.—Of these, how shall I speak both briefly enough and greatly enough? They are just this — to be like Him whom not having seen, we love"; to displace accordingly, in grave reality, self from the inner throne, and to enthrone Him; to make not the slightest compromise with the smallest sin. We aim to be entirely willing, nay, definitely to will, to know with ever keener sensibility what

_{1 Pet. i. 8.}

is sin in us, and where it is, that it may be dealt with at once by the Holy Spirit. We aim at nothing less than to walk with God all day long; to abide every hour in Christ, and He and His words in us; to love God with all the heart, and our neighbour as ourselves; to live, and that in no conventional sense, "no longer to ourselves, but to Him who died for us, and rose again." We aim to "yield ourselves to God" as the unregenerate will yields itself to sin, to self; to have "every thought brought into captivity to the obedience of Christ"— every thought, every movement of the inner world; a strict, comprehensive captivity, an absolute and arbitrary slavery. In the region of outward life our aim is, of course, equally large and pervading. It is to break with all evil, and follow all good. It is never, never more to speak evil of any man; never to lose patience; never

Joh. xv. 7.

Matt. xxii 37, 39.

2 Cor. v. 15.

Rom. vi. 13.

2 Cor. x. 5.

to trifle with wrong, whether impurity, untruth, or unkindness; never in any known thing to evade our Master's will; never to be ashamed of His name. I emphasize again and again this "never," for there is the point. As believers in our Lord Jesus Christ, as those who are not their own, but bought, and who accordingly, in the strictest sense, belong to Him all through, our aim is, it must be, across any amount of counterthoughts, "never to grieve Him, never to stray"; always in the inner world, always in the outer, to "walk and to please Him." I say again, this is our aim, not in any conventional sense, such as to leave us easy and tolerably comfortable when we fail. Not so; God forbid. Failure, when it comes across this aim, will come with the pang of a shame and disappointment which we shall little wish to feel again. It will be a deeply conscious discord and

1 Thess. iv. 1.

collision. It will be a fall down a rough steep. It will be a joy lost, or, at best, deferred again. It will be the missing of a divine smile, the loss of "the light of the countenance of the King." Prov. xvi. 15.

Let me repeat it, even to the risk of weariness; the Christian's aim is bound, absolutely bound, to be nothing less than this—"Let the words of my lips, and the meditation of my heart, be always acceptable in Thy sight, O Lord, my Rock and my Redeemer." We are absolutely bound Ps xix. 14. to put quite aside all secret purposes of moral compromise; all tolerance of besetting sin, for the sad reason that it is besetting. With open face we behold the glory of the Lord, and ask to be changed 2 Cor. iii. 18. at any cost, all round the circle of life, into the same image. We cannot possibly rest short of a daily, hourly, continuous walk with God, in Christ, by the grace of the Holy Ghost.

2. But I come to speak briefly of the LIMITS. I will not dwell upon them, but I must indicate them. I mean, of course, not limits in our aims, for there must be none, nor limits in divine grace itself, for there are none, but limits, however caused, in the actual attainment by us of Christian holiness. Here I hold, with absolute conviction, alike from the experience of the Church and from the infallible Word, that, in the mystery of things, there will be limits to the last, and very humbling limits, very real fallings short. To the last, it will be *a Sinner* that walks with God. To the last will " abide in the regenerate" (Art. ix.) that strange tendency, that " mind of the flesh," which eternal grace can wonderfully deal with, but which is a tendency still. To the last, the soul's acceptance before the JUDGE is wholly and only in the righteousness, the merits, of Christ. To the last, if we

say we have no sin, we deceive ourselves. 1 Joh. i. 8. In the pure warm sunshine of the Father's smile shed upon the loving and willing *child*, that child will yet say, "Enter not into judgment with thy *servant*." Walking in the light as He is Ps. cxliii. 2. in the light, having fellowship with Him, and He with us, we yet need to the last 1 Joh. i. 7. the blood of Calvary, the blood of propitiation, to deal with sin.*

I shall scarcely revert to this side of truth as we proceed, for my aim is at present towards the other pole. But let me thus once for all enter a humble warning against the error and danger of explaining away the Word of God when it tells of an ever-abiding need, in the believer's life, of confession of sin.

3. Then, lastly, come up into view the

---

* This aspect of truth is discussed more fully in the Author's Treatise, "Justifying Righteousness." London : Seeley & Co.

sacred POSSIBILITIES of the matter. A submissive recognition of limits will only help us to grasp these with the more hope and joy.

It is possible, I dare to say, for those who will indeed draw on their Lord's power for deliverance and victory, to live a life—how shall I describe it?—a life in which His promises are taken as they stand, and found to be true. It is possible to cast *every* care on Him, daily, and to be at peace amidst the pressure. It is possible to have affections and imaginations purified through faith, in a profound and practical sense. It is possible to see the will of God in everything, and to find it, as one has said, no longer a sigh, but a song. It is possible, in the world of inner act and motion, to put away, to get put away, *all* bitterness, and wrath, and anger, and evil speaking, daily and hourly. It is possible, by unreserved

Eph. iv. 31.

resort to divine power, under divine conditions, to become strongest, through and through, at our weakest point; to find the thing which yesterday upset all our obligations to patience, or to purity, or to humility, an occasion to-day, through Him who loveth us, and worketh in us, for a joyful consent to His will, and a delightful sense of His presence and sin-annulling power. These are things divinely possible. And, because they are His work, the genuine experience of them will lay us, must lay us, only lower at His feet, and leave us only more athirst for more.

Some of the conditions of such experience we will consider in the next chapter.

Meanwhile, may I ask each reader of these pages to pause here, with the heart-question, How high goes my own conscious aim, and, what, as to the possibilities of grace, are my personal expectations? And will he add a prayer? "Thou, Lord, who knowest my heart, all its desire and all its need, show me what Thou art able to do with it, and do what Thou art able; through Jesus Christ. Amen."

II.

SELF-DENIAL AND THE DAILY CROSS.

WE have reviewed some of the Possibilities of the believer's life, as a life in which the promises of God are taken as they stand, and found to be true. We may just so far linger over this side of the great truth before us as to make a reflection at once humiliating and encouraging; the reflection that no one definite act of sinning, as I look back upon it, need have taken place. Every act of sinning, yes, down to the sin of acts of thought, or states of thought, displeasing to God, is a *contradiction to first principles of the Gospel.* Put the case of those inner emotions of wrong which seem most to defy repression. Take the last transient swell of petty impatience, or of unkind criticism; things which, to the unawakened conscience, look so small, to the awakened conscience, so large. There is not one that need have taken place. To me, as a living and believing member of Christ, resources are always open which can anticipate and prevent these things. Had I been walking that moment with God, abiding that moment in Christ, drawing that moment on the sanctifying Spirit's power, I should not have lost temper, I should not have thought unkindly: not only should I not have *lookea* impatience, or indulged in needless severity of *words*. The occasion for the very feeling would have been as if it were not, because neutralized in Jesus Christ. And if that might have been true for the last five minutes, why should it not be true for the next five, for the present minute?

"I can do all things," I have resources for all circumstances, "in Him that strength-eneth me." *Phil. iv. 13.*

But already the earnest soul, athirst for a personal experience of what we have been depicting, has asked itself, How shall I, with my thousand difficulties, get what I thirst for? In the present chapter we will try to deal with the one difficulty that underlies the thousand. That difficulty is "Self." And Self-*denial* is the first condition to this life of calm and humble spiritual victory, or better call it, spiritual deliverance.

It is no unconditional thing. Right and left, the highway of holiness has its edge, its limit, its *sine quâ non*. On the one hand, the Lord, and childlike trust in Him and in His words. On the other hand, amongst other things, but supreme amongst them, Self-denial and the daily Cross. Of the Lord Himself we shall speak more directly in future pages. At present I look the other way, believing that this order may be most helpful for solidity of thought.

"If any man will come, willeth to to come, after Me, let him deny himself, and take up his cross daily, and follow Me." Let us study these familiar words a little in detail.

<small>Luke ix. 23.</small>

1. Observe the universality of reference. "If *any* man wills to come after Me; whoever desires to follow My lead; then let this man, be he who he may, do thus: Let him deny himself, and daily take up his cross, and follow Me. Let any man who wills to follow Me, and does not do thus, by no means marvel if his following, such as it is, proves to be a disappointing, a disheartening thing. Let such a one prepare to find My yoke uneasy, and My burden heavy, and My commandments grievous."

2. Then "let him deny *himself*." Always let us emphasize, in thought and in tone, that last word, "let him deny *himself*." And what is *Self*-denial? The word is often and much mistaken in common use, as if it meant much the same as self-control—the control of lower elements of our being by higher. If a man postpones the present to the future, resolving on present loss for the sake of future gain, this is often called Self-denial. If a man, for some high object of his own, abjures inferior pleasures, "scorns delights, and lives laborious days," this is often called Self-denial. If, in the highest sphere, for the sake of rest hereafter, he inflicts on himself great unrest now, this too is often called Self-denial.

Now the doing of such things may be wrong or may be right in itself; but it is not self-denial, as the phrase is used here assuredly by our Lord. Take the New

Testament and try the case by the words "deny," "denial," in successive passages; I think it will be seen that self-denial is not self-control. In all cases at all in point, "to deny" much more resembles in idea "to ignore" than "to control." It means to turn the back upon, to shut the eyes to, to treat as non-existent. "I will deny him"; I will say, I know him not. "He cannot deny Himself"; He cannot ignore His own hand in His own written promise. "Let him deny himself"; let him ignore self; let him say to self, I know thee not, thou art nothing to me.

<small>Matt. x. 33.
2 Tim. ii. 13.</small>

In effect, may we not say, the Lord's precept comes to this—the real displacement of self from the throne of life in its purposes and hopes, and the real enthronement of Another. It comes to—unqualified self-surrender. I attempt no refinements. We all practically understand what we mean when we speak about self and its surrender, and the enthronement of Jesus Christ. We mean that whereas yesterday our aims, many of them, some of them, one of them, terminated in ourself, to-day, so far as we know, they all terminate in our Lord. Yesterday, perhaps in some highly refined mode, perhaps in some mode not refined, we lived at least a part of our life to self; now, in full purpose, we live the whole of it to Him who died for us and rose again. Yesterday it was very pleasant, as a good thing in itself, if some action, some influence going out from us, brought back praise, spoken or not spoken, to ourselves; now such a feeling is recognized as sin, if the pleasure terminates short of a distinct and honest reference to our Lord in us. Yesterday we were easy in the consciousness of purely personal gratification, when some intellectual success, let us say, or physical, brought credit to ourselves and stimulated self-esteem. Oh, how much inner force have we spent in one phase or another of self-esteem! But to-day our deliberate choice is in the other direction. We prefer, with unaffected preference, that all our earnings should go straight to another, to our Lord. In true purpose and choice He is now the centre of our whole life; not of parts, but of the whole. We wish not to spend ten minutes *irrespective* of His interests, His claims, His will.

This is the self-denial of the saints. It is no fanatical, no visionary thing. It does not mean a mechanical asceticism. It does not, of any necessity in itself, contradict or condemn the most natural activities and interests of human life, as such. It does not absorb nor cancel personality. Rather this is the very thing to enrich the resources of personal being, and to develop its exercises. But it has lodged it, as to its whole purpose and working, *upon another centre,* even Jesus Christ the Lord.

I need not follow the line of thought further into detail. Each heart will do this best for itself. It is a long line, for it has a deep sea to fathom.

3. "And let him take up his cross daily, and follow Me." Every word is pregnant here, the "taking up"—the acceptance by the regenerate will, with a true surrender, of whatever may be meant by the cross! And then, the "cross"! Observe, it is not the yoke, the burden, but the *Cross*—a word of very definite imagery; a thing to be carried indeed, as any burden is to be carried— but whither, and why? To a Calvary, and because of a Crucifixion to be done there. The "self" just "denied," just ignored, rejected, is to be also bound and

nailed as to a Roman cross, and this with the consenting act of the regenerate will, which has taken up that cross for that end. And then, "daily"! Therefore, for one thing, there is a somewhat to be daily crucified. Here is one inexhaustible paradox of this great matter; on one side a true and total self-denial, on the other, a daily need of self-crucifixion. This is a thing which I am content simply to state, and to leave it as the Lord's word upon the believer's mind and soul.

But "*daily*"; without intermission, without holiday; now, to-day, this hour; and then, to-morrow! And the daily "*cross*"; a something which is to be the instrument of disgrace and execution to something else! And what will that something be? Just whatever gives occasion of ever deeper test to the Self-surrender of which we have spoken; just whatever exposes to shame and death the old aims, and purposes, and plans, the old spirit of Self and its life.

Perhaps some great anguish on another's behalf threatens you. Yesterday you shrank from it, you stumbled at it, very largely, if not mainly, because of what it would inflict on Self. To-day you *take it up,* as a cross, and upon it you execute that thought; and now your pain is pure pain, pain for the sake of another's soul, and of the glory of God.

Perhaps it is some small trifle of daily routine; a crossing of personal preference in very little things; accumulation of duties, unexpected interruption, unwelcome distraction. Yesterday these things merely fretted you and, internally at least, " *upset* " you. To-day, on the contrary, you *take them up,* and stretch your hands out upon them, and let them be the occasion of new disgrace and deeper death for that old self-spirit. You take them up in loving, worshipping acceptance. You carry them to their Calvary in thankful submission. And to-morrow you will do the same.

4. " And let him follow Me." This may refer specially to the last previous words, the Cross-bearing; it may betoken a following of Him, who "went out bearing His Cross." But it may better be referred to the whole previous verse, to that mysterious Self-denial of the Son, whereby, throughout His blessed course, " His meat was to do, not His own will, but the will of Him that sent Him," and " to glorify Him on the earth." Thus we have more in view than the final " going out " to Calvary.

<small>Joh. iv. 34.
Joh. xvii 4.</small>

In any case, let the disciple do all this always, wholly, with regard to Him, looking unto Him, " following Him."

I leave upon the heart, with little attempt at system, just this utterance of the Christian's Master calling His bondservant out to the path of holiness. Listen, weigh, and apply to the inmost self. Let the cost be counted before the results are claimed. Would you know what it is, in the strong but gentle realities of a happy experience, to be "he that overcometh," to have "heart and thoughts kept by the peace of God"? Then more is needed than even the holiest aspirations. There needs certain definite demands on the regenerate will. You must draw for every victory upon divine resources. But you must do it as one who is, in full heart-purpose, self-surrendered, denying the life of self, and daily taking up the cross. In the next chapter we will consider how we are to do this with self.

_{Rev. iii. 5.}
_{Phil. iv. 7.}

III.

GOD IS ABLE.

We have just dealt specially with the dethronement of self and the daily acceptance of its crucifixion; speaking thus early of this side of truth, in the conviction that the soul, seeking a closer conformity to the will of God, needs very definitely to ask itself at the outset—whether its present attitude is one of true receptivity; whether it not only believes that "He is able," but is willing that He should put His ability into definite action at any cost to self.

We shall now as we proceed bend our thoughts more directly upon the Lord Himself, in some of those glorious character in which He is "made to us Sanctification": and this, I am sure, will be

1 Cor. i. 30.

in the proportion of the Gospel. We must look far more at Him than at our attitude towards Him. In Baxter's well-known words, we must take ten looks at Christ for one at self. But none the less it is well to look early in the process of thought, and to look decisively, at what is the attitude of our will towards Him. If that is not done, interminable disappointment is a sad probability, where the Holy Spirit keeps conscience awake so as to feel it.

Before coming to a view, somewhat in detail, of one or another of the characters of Christ as our Sanctification, let us here pause awhile before the grand fact in general that He, this Being who indeed is not ourselves, is able to deal with us in our inmost self, and has announced His willingness to do it. Leave alone for the moment analysis and theory, however true, and ponder the FACT. Is it not good to do so, after such views as we have just been taking? We have held up to our own eyes an ideal of the life of walk with God, with a distinct resolve that it shall not remain for us a mere ideal. It shall be translated and transfigured into the real. It shall be, in some true and solid sense, reflected, before God and before man, in our experience and our life. Never, we know, will this ideal and this real absolutely coincide in our mortal state; if only for this reason, that we shall not be "like Him," absolutely, till "we see Him as He is." But then, we may be very much more like Him, relatively, than we are. We may reach to-day such a new development of likeness that it may be, to what was in us yesterday, a realization of the ideal, though to-morrow may bring in its turn what shall put to-day to shame. Such, however, has been our thought in the opening chapter.

1 Joh. iii. 2.

And then, in what followed, we gazed upon some of the conditions of the attainment; self-denial and the daily cross.

Now is not one first result of such views, a deeper and keener sense than ever of self-impotency? Noble and beautiful ideal! Just and conscience-waking conditions! But, am I not where I was before, only more aware of it? Are you not asking me to do precisely what is impossible, that I may enter upon a life of peace and spiritual power; to step on to this rock of strength, this lap of rest, across a gulf I cannot leap, and while I have no wings? Can self deny self? Can the centre of my acts and thoughts dislodge itself? Can I will that for which I am unwilling? Can I spring away, once and for all, from my own shadow?

In reply to such heart-questionings we will be perfectly practical. The heart, rather than the pure reason, is the questioner in this matter; and words which God has spoken in Scripture to the heart will be the best reply.

Do you remember the instructive progress of the Psalmist's thought, Psalm xlii. 4, 5, 6? He is in sore perplexity, and he is athirst for God. At first, he "pours out his soul in him," or better, perhaps, "upon him"; throws and leans his distress upon himself, in weary introspection. Then, he reasons with that "soul"; conjures it not to "fret upon him"; entreats it to look up and off to God. Then, better still, he leaves this internal analysis and debate, and speaks direct to God, to his God; "O my God, my soul is cast down within me; therefore will I REMEMBER THEE."

This saint of old shall be our guide. We will "REMEMBER HIM." We will leave the anxious metaphysics of the inner man, and we will go out and up, in some quiet, steady, recollections of fact. "O my God, I will remember Thee."

Think then of this great, pervading, phenomenon of Scripture—its presentation of the LORD Himself,—in His infinite but personal Being, outside mine, though the source and base of mine still, —as able to deal with me, to work in me, to work through me. Gather together such utterances as these, and believe them as you read them :—" He is able to do exceeding abundantly, above what we ask or think, according to the power that worketh in us"; "My grace is sufficient for thee ; My strength is made perfect in weakness"; "Thou wilt keep him in perfect peace, whose mind is stayed on Thee"; "They that wait on the Lord shall renew their strength"; "With Thee is the fountain of life"; "I am come that they might have life"; "I

Eph. iii. 20.
2 Cor. xii. 9.
Isa. xxvi. 3.
Isa. xl. 31.
Psa. xxxvi 9.
Joh. x. 10, 28.

give eternal life"; "He is able to save to the uttermost them that come unto God by Him"; "He is able to keep what I have committed unto Him"; "He is able to make all grace abound towards you"; "He is able to keep you from falling"; "He is faithful"; "He worketh in you, to will and to do"; "The life I live in the flesh, I live by faith in the Son of God"; "Not I, but Christ liveth in me"; "Not I, but the grace of God with me"; "Much more, being reconciled by the death of the Son of God, we shall be saved in His life"; "The very God of peace sanctify you throughout"; "The God of peace, who brought again the great Shepherd, make you perfect," equip, or *adjust*, you perfectly, "to do His will, working in you that which is well-pleasing in His sight."

Now, mark, these are but some great clusters from the valleys of the Scripture

Marginal references: Heb. vii. 25. 2 Tim. i. 12. 2 Cor. ix. 8. Jude 24. Heb. x. 23. Phil. ii. 13. Gal. ii. 20. 1 Cor. xv. 10. Rom. v. 10. 1 Thess. v. 23. Heb. xiii. 20, 21.

God is Able. 41

Canaan. But are not these enough to show that "with God *all things*," all things proposed to faith, "are possible," however impossible in themselves? Looking at these words of the living God, will you not take in, and ever more take in, the divine certainty that "HE IS ABLE," and write it across every practical problem of the first step, and the next step, of your walk with God by faith?

Yes, clasp this side, the *not-self* side, of the Scripture promises. Fear not lest the legitimate action of self, of you, should be unduly eliminated. With the heart that asks the questions we have supposed, that is the last risk, and the least. What you need is to look away to this eternal Person undertaking for you, even before you ask in any detail what He says about His mode of action.

Read again, all through your Bible, your infallible Bible, the places that give you this view of Him. Are they trite to you, are they *passé?* In honesty with yourself, have you to own that "the glory is departed from them" which once, perhaps, shone so richly from them? Believe me, if heart answereth to heart, I know the reason. It is because you have ceased to expect them to act. It is because you have been willing to put your own conventional gloss upon them. It is because you have assumed words to refer wholly to an indefinite future, and another order of things, which are meant to be "words of eternal life" for the experience of to-day. What is meant to be your plank at this moment in the deep flood, you have taken to be only the distant shore to which, practically unaided, you are to swim, half-drowned.

"O my God, I will remember THEE. Thou art not myself. Thou knowest me far better than I know myself. I cannot deal with that self; but Thou art able. I cannot manipulate the '*springs of thought and will*'; but Thou art able. Though I can indeed, with the powers Thou hast given me as man, do certain things in modification of action, yet I cannot, no, I cannot, break habits decisively and at their root. But Thou art able. Thou knowest all that besets me; Thou knowest my circumstances; Thou 'knowest where I dwell;' Thou art acquainted with every element in my character, my temperament, that responds to the besetments of my position. And Thou, infinitely real and truly personal, art able to handle me throughout, in some wonderful way of Thine own, with a divine personal influence, to which it must indeed be blessed to submit. Take Thou me in hand. I am indeed a difficult problem, insoluble to myself, but not to Thee. The more baffling the moral

Rev. ii. 13.

difficulty, the more inveterate the habit, the more will be shown Thy skill in dealing with it. Be THOU magnified in my body, and in my spirit, which are Thine. I yield myself to Thee."

Yes, our deepest need, when the heart is alive with desire, and conscious of impotence, is first to realize, and then to submit to, Him of whom "it is witnessed that He liveth." Heb. vii. 8

"He that sitteth upon the throne saith, Behold, I make all things new." That is true not for the Universe only, nor for the Church only, but for the individual, for thee; and not for the eternal future only, but for the present; for the disorder of the soul, of thy soul, to-day. It is the KING who speaks, sitting on the throne. See Him as such, come to Him as such; and expect to find, in the depths of being, and even now, that God is true, and God is able.

[marginal refs: Heb. vii. 8; Rev. xxi. 5.]

IV.

THE DIVINE MASTER.

We are turning our thoughts directly to the Lord Jesus Christ Himself, as the secret of all Christian Holiness. The infinitely sacred subject can only be touched, and that only at a very few of its countless salient points. Intentionally I shall avoid many aspects, even paramount aspects, of the truth as it is in Jesus. I will but allude in passing to the Saviour as my Justification, my Sacrifice of peace, my Righteousness before the Holy God. And I will but thus passingly allude to Him, for the present, as the great Firstborn among many brethren, the Second Man, the Root and Life-spring of the New Race, of New Men, of New Man.

<small>Rom. viii. 29.
1 Cor. xv. 47.</small>

I would take just now these great underlying truths for granted. Let us come, carrying them always in the heart, to some of those holy phenomena of the surface, if I may so speak, which will be more immediately present to the conciousness of him, who in self-dedication, and in simplicity of faith, steps out in an hourly walk with God.

So now first I reverently place my Redeemer before me as my MASTER.

This aspect of His sacred Personality towards me comes thus first in the order of thought about Him, by no means at random. We hope to consider Him ere long as the Keeper, and as the Friend; and how many other titles might we not gather round His Name, full of tenderness unspeakable! But if we would get aright at these, for use in the hourly path, for rest amid overwhelming pressure or interlacing cares, or for the spiritual mind amidst the common intercourse of common days, sure I am—deeply sure—that we need to lay beneath all these restful views of Christ, and to weave as a thread of strength and truth into them all, the thought, the fact, that He is the Master, the Master of a veritable slave, and that slave here, now, always, everywhere, myself.

True, there are texts in which the Lord and His Apostles waive this idea for a special purpose. "I call you not servants, but friends"; "Thou art no more a servant, but a son." But a little attention shows that we have in such sentences, as often in Scripture, one side of truth isolated and spoken of absolutely, while yet other sides hold good. He who calls His followers friends, says on the same occasion that they do well to

<small>Joh. xv 15.
Gal. iv. 7</small>

call Him Lord. And soon He deals with them as Lord indeed: "If I will that he tarry till I come, what is that to thee?" And the Apostle who bids the believer repudiate in one respect the idea of bondage, clasps it in another to his inmost soul: "Paul, the slave of Jesus Christ"; "Whose I am"; "Enslaved to God."

Thus the idea is a permanent one, so permanent that it is carried on into the eternal state: "His bond-servants shall serve Him, and they shall see His face."

And what I deeply feel and would earnestly enforce with regard to this idea, is that it is an idea precisely fit to give safety and solidity to every tenderer one. Fail to recognize it to the full, fail of an unreserved and habitual recognition that this is my despotic Master, a recognition carried into the inner habit of every-day thought and purpose, and there will be in every other aspect of Jesus Christ to me a something out of order, a lack of fixity, a lack of rest.

It is deeply significant that His own blessed invitation to the weary and the heavy laden, speaks at once of a yoke and a burden. How shall you find rest unto your souls? How shall you understand that I am meek and lowly of heart? Take My yoke upon you; become one of My "servants under the yoke." So, and not otherwise, you shall understand. *Matt. xi. 28, 29.* *1 Tim. vi. 1.*

Let me look then every day and hour, and, as to the mental *habit*, every moment, upon Jesus Christ as my Master. Saintly George Herbert chose that to be, as it were, his best-beloved aspect of his Saviour: "My Master, Jesus"; "An oriental fragrancy, my Master."* Let me do the same. Let me wear the word next the heart, next the will; nay, let it sink into the very springs of both, deeper every day.

* "*The Odour.*"

Let me get up every morning with this for the instantaneous thought, that my Master wakes me. I wake, I rise, His property. Before I go out to plough or feed, or whatever it may be, upon His domain, let me with reverent and deep joy go into His private chamber, as it were, and avow Him as my Master, my Possessor; absolute, not constitutional; supremely entitled to order me about all day, and, if He pleases, not to thank me at the close. Let me put the neck of self beneath His feet, and rise up bearing, not the cross only, which is another thought, but the yoke, the implement of menial service, the pledge of readiness to do and to carry anything. And let me continually, in the habit of my thought, be coming again into that Presence-chamber, to renew the act of that dedication and submission. With each call and claim the day may bring, let me carry into all things, let me have ready for them, this "oriental fragrancy, my Master." Is it regulated and expected duty? How delightful the thought that hands, or head, or voice, are indeed the implements of the faithful slave, kept at work for such an Owner! Is it unlooked-for and additional service? It is the Master's sudden call, I am wanted, and it is by Him. Let me rise with alacrity at His lightest bidding, and ask His pleasure. Is it the miscellaneous intercourse of life? Let my mental habit be so full of "my Master," that I shall be on the watch, always and everywhere, to be used by Him, or to "stand and wait" close to Him, as He pleases; only always knowing myself to be His property, and glad indeed so to be. Let others always know "where to find me," as the phrase is; because I am bound and anchored to His blessed will by the realized and heart-welcomed fact of this thrice-holy, entire, and literal slavery.

Yes, and let me remember and welcome down into the depths of my being the fact that His despotism is above all things to be felt *there*. In my *innermost self* I have no personal rights against Him. Every thought is a lawful captive and slave to Him. No corner of that mysterious world, my spirit, no movement of will, or of desire, has a right to be other than He wills. I am bound, fast bound, to think as He does, to like and dislike with Him, to lay every personal prejudice and pique and so-called just sensibility on self's part beneath His despotic foot; and to leave it there, looking to Him to keep it down all day long. Let me never for one minute be content with the externals, however real in their sphere, of submission and of bondage. No; I am bound from within, from the depths. So it was

1 Cor. x. 5.

of old when I lived that self-life I now deplore. The will was not free to righteousness; it was a *servum arbitrium*, a slave-will, *that* way; and it was bound from within. Now it is not free to evil. It is a slave-will *that* way, and it is bound from within; for a Master, a despotic Possessor, dwells in my heart by faith. He says no. It is against orders. And the orders speak now in the region where to speak is to control.

So I take His yoke upon me, and I ask Him never to let me take it off; no, not for a minute. My gracious "Master still bestows needful periods of repose." He knows my frame. But when that repose does come, perhaps in some vigorous re-creation in my youth, perhaps in calmer wise in maturer years, by shore or forest, on field or mountain, it is not for one moment release from slavery. The inner despotism is as merciful and as real as

Ps. ciii 14.

ever; and as to outward service, I am ever to stand ready for it. My Master has but sent me for renewal of strength to some fair corner of His domain, never off it; and will often meet me there, and remind me what I am, and may bid me work for Him there, if He sees it right. And He expects me to go back to the task when the rest is over, with all the blessedness of a renewed and absolute avowal of what I am, and for whom I live; "an oriental fragrancy, my Master."

And just the same it will be if He lays me low with sickness, accident, agony; bids me seemingly be useless for Him. Has He done it? I am to ask no questions. Not for a moment am I a self-determining being. "Yes, Master; I know what I am, and I know Thee, and Thou knowest me, and knowest best."

Very feebly have I tried to sketch some

practical, not sentimental, exercises of thought and will upon those stern, those merciful words, Master, Despot, Slave. May I dare to say they have become in growing realization blessed realities to myself? Ah! how imperfectly grasped yet; but enough to justify me, a sinner, in venturing to say, "Taste and see that this Master, this unutterably real and despotic Master, is good. There *is* rest here for the soul."

It may seem strange to quote Aristotle in connexion with Christian sanctity. But there is a passage on slavery in the *Politics*, at the opening, which I have lately read after many years with deep interest and emotion. It is a ruthless statement of the principles of bond-service of man to man, but we can read into it the golden gloss of the bond-service of redeemed man to Jesus Christ. What is Aristotle's account of "nature's own slave," the being meant for bondage? He **is** "a chattel that lives"; he is "a part of his master; as it were a living, though separated, portion of his body." He has, strictly speaking, no existence apart from his master; he is "not only the slave of the master, but the master's, wholly his"; so that, in no action or relation of life, is he for one moment an independent being. On the other hand—how finely and truly said!—there is thus and therefore between the born master and the born slave a relation of common interest and mutual friendship.

Are we not reminded by the way of that rule of the Passover, which entitled the born or purchased bond-servant to share the holy meal with his master, but shut out the hired servant altogether?

Ex. xiii. 44, 45.

Surely, in this page of Aristotle we read, we find expressed to the letter, almost to the spirit, the relation between the Christian and Christ. The servant is his master's piece of absolute property.

He is a part of his Master. He has no foothold for a moment's independence. He is, as a "slave by nature," by new nature, near to his Master, in closest interest and in reverent friendship.

And further, still in Aristotle's words scarcely modified, "he is by nature a slave, as one made to belong to another, and as sharing that other's mind so far as to perceive it." Yes, after all, the slave of Christ, though purchased and branded for a most literal servitude, is made capable of a true perception of his Master's mind, a sympathy, as true as it is humble, with his Master's will, an intuition into his Master's wish. And thus it is his delightful privilege evermore to act *as if* free, in just this respect, that he can look in his Master's face and say, as one who is at liberty to go if he will, "I love Thee, I am well with Thee, I will not go out free." Ex. xxi. 5.

V.

THE DIVINE KEEPER.

WE were occupied in the last chapter with the thought of the Divine Master. We viewed the Lord Jesus Christ under the special character of the absolute and despotic Owner of the spirit, soul, and body, of His purchased and self-dedicated servant. We recalled, in the last words, that interesting detail in the law of Hebrew bond-service, in which the slave, whose year of release had arrived, might of his own choice elect to be a slave for ever; "I am well with Thee, I will not go out free." His master thereupon pierced his ear, fastening it for the moment to the house-door, a pledge and brand of perpetual connexion with the house, and

(margin: Ex. xxi. 5; Deut. xv. 16.)

perpetual obedience. Delightful parable of what the Christian may, not once only, but evermore, be doing in his conscious relations with his divine and beloved Possessor! "O my Master, I have felt Thy yoke. I have tried Thy despotism, deep within my soul as well as in the outside of my life. It is real, intensely real, stricter and more penetrating by far than any other ownership can be. I see that it means for me the continuous surrender to Thee, in full reality, of all I am, and all I have and do. But I have found in it the glorious paradox of a blissful and restful liberty. I have found the secret of a nearness to Thee and fellowship with Thee unfelt before. I know my absolute Sovereign to be, while He never relaxes His sovereignty for a moment, yet meek and lowly in heart, as I could not know it before. I have begun to taste the deep sweetness of a life whose sole inner aim is to be a vessel for the Master's use, when and how He pleases. And so it is well with me in Thy bondage. Brand me again. Bind me to Thy house-work again. I will not go out free."

<small>2 Tim. ii. 21.</small>

We shall never get beyond the occasion of such new surrenders, nor beyond their blessedness. Every day, and well nigh every thing, may give the opportunity. Sharpest trials, deepest repose; the Lord's takings and the Lord's givings; things which definitely remind us of slavery, things which largely tempt us to forget it, or to conceal it; all will give us opportunity, which we will rejoice to take. Through such renewals of our surrender, if they are done in truth of heart before Him, will flow in very markedly indeed the sanctifying powers of our Master's life, the precious influences of our mystical union with our glorious Head.

The Divine Keeper.

Realize deliberately, and in fact, that you are the slave of Jesus Christ. Blessed position! How different from that of a passing visitor with Him; a traveller through His land, stopping at pleasure to sketch or measure it! Such are not you; bound to the soil, or rather to its Lord; with ceaseless obligations there; indissoluble relations to Him; a very real piece of His property, and so, of very real concern to Him.

And here may naturally come in our new topic, the divine Keeper. As before, we take up a revealed relation between the Lord and the believer, with special view to its bearing on Christian holiness. Let us think a little, in this aspect, of the keeping power of Christ.

I have realized, then, that I am His property, His implement for use, His living chattel, in the words quoted above (p. 11) from Aristotle's account of slavery. True, I always *am* such. But in a true sense I also *become* such in each crisis, now in this last crisis, of self-surrender. I have renounced, definitely renounced, the aims of the old life of self, and, among them, its aim to govern itself, in its own name, more or less wisely and successfully. And now what has happened correspondingly? This divine Possessor, who now, in a sense so true and special, holds me as not my own but His, assuredly regards me, and thinks of me in a sense correspondingly special, as a piece of instrumental property and possession, to be used, and therefore to be kept. His word encourages me to this view, not my fancy or reverie. The man who through grace has " purged himself from these," separating himself from the life of sin, that is of self, to God, is revealed to be *ipso facto* " a vessel for the Master's use " and

<small>2 Tim. ii. 21.</small>

what a master uses, will he not, for himself, from his own point of view, take care of? Will it not concern him to keep it near him, to keep it in order, to keep it clean?

You see the suggestion of thought. In the fact of that self-disfranchisement on my part, which God secures, and also invites, there lies imbedded a holy further fact, that the Master who owns me will very specially take care of me. And He will do this in all the respects in which, for His purposes, I need it. For let me think for the while, as far as I can, of *His* point of view only. *For His purposes* He will take very special care of me indeed. And of all respects in which this care will be taken, which may I fix upon with most certainty, most expectation, most realization? Surely that which concerns my inner man; my world of thought and will, the seat and spring of all that comes out in external service, and according to the attitude of which towards Him will be the whole character—in His sight—of that external service. I am an instrument for His use; perhaps to bear burdens, as of pain, sorrow, or shame; perhaps to convey messages, writing, speaking, conversing; perhaps simply to reflect light, showing His mind in the commonest of all daily rounds. In only one way can I truly do anything of these; in the way of inner harmony with Him, and peace and joy in Him. Will He not now take care, in a very special way, of this for me? Yes, He surely will. Let me keep the two thoughts, or rather the two facts, the two realities, in connexion—the Ownership and the Keeping; the Owner and the Keeper—one dear and sovereign Lord;—and I shall not be disappointed in the latter. Let go the former;

wish to be my own, claim to be—however partially—my own; and let me not look for the Master's keeping of the unfit instrument. Something else will be needed for it; perhaps, for a time, some sternly merciful taking to pieces; but not this sacred keeping. But accept Him wholly, in the sense of our last chapter, as Master, and we shall know something of it indeed.

I am not about to enter on any elaborate discussion of the relations between our will and the Lord's. No; I would only say that certain broad facts on this great subject stand out in the Word of God, never to be forgotten. One is, the true and permanent reality of my will. It is never viewed as exhaled, or absorbed, into the will of God, but as willingly yielded to it, a very different thing. And when so yielded, it is still to be employed, with holy reality and activity; only in very different directions, probably, and with very different aims from of old. It will *will*, for instance, in temptation far rather to call in the Master's strength than to employ the forces, such as they are, of my own introspections, and reasonings, and resolves. Yes, my will remains real and acting. But then, on the other hand, the Scripture makes it plain, perhaps much plainer than I once thought, that His will on me and in me is an immense reality; His will, personal, external to me, operative, effectual, trustworthy beyond all words. It tells me, and perhaps it comes to me with the light of a new world, a new sun of calm pure light and heat, that this Personal Being, whose I am, is ready, if I will trust Him for it, to act on me and in me with a present power of divine life and personal influence which is able to do great things, whereof I shall be glad; able so to do them that, if I may dare to say so, it shall be *as if, as if,* the victory over temptation, the deliverance from sinning, the animation to love, the leading forth to witness and labour, were the independent and isolated action in me of another, of my Master and Keeper. Nay, I am so to realize Him in this mighty "not-myself" of His will and work as to trust Him, (while I maintain the attitude of His slave, His chattel,) for innumerable modes of purifying and preserving power in me and on me, quite beyond my analysis. I only know about them all that they are ministered to me by the Blessed Spirit, through Whom I and my Lord are one. But I am content to know this, and no more, in accepting the soul-blessing realization that "His grace," not will be, may be, but "IS SUFFICIENT for me"; that He is able to keep me from falling; that I am kept by

2 Cor. xii 9. Jude 24.

His Father's power; that His power worketh in me; that He can keep me back from sins; keep me in perfect peace; keep that which I have committed unto Him;—and into His hands have I committed my spirit, not for death only but for life, for the present hour.

" Able to keep." I know well how liable is this blissful truth, like every other, to distortions and misuse. It is possible so to state it, or rather so to ignore other truth beside it, as almost to deny our immortal personality, or our present responsibility. It is possible so to interpret "not I, but Christ," as that it shall come strangely round, in practical result, to mean, " not Christ, but I." But sure I am that this truth, liable to *mis*use, is more liable to *dis*use. And so I venture to state it and to press it, for the once, unbalanced and unrelieved. Commit, O bond-servant of Christ Jesus,

The Divine Keeper. 69

the keeping of thy spirit unto Him. In the problem of internal evil, in face of the dark and abiding fact of internal evil, in the question what to do with that which in thee ever tends to come up and out in vanity, in envy, in impurity, in anger, in levity, in self-indulgence, in selfishness of every shade, in actions of evil and absences of good—throw thy will supremely in the direction of looking off from the temptation, and unto Him, and commit to Him the keeping. Thou absolutely belongest unto Him, His slave, His implement, for His work. He is not only able, He greatly cares, to keep thy spirit. And do not stay to analyse how, in the crisis of need. He knows well how to act; according to the mighty working whereby He is able to subdue even all things to Himself. And be sure that these acts of peace-bringing trust will result, by His gracious will, in a holy

Phil. iii. 21.

deepening attitude and habit; in the gaze, instinctive, willing, restful, of "eyes that are *ever* toward the Lord; for HE shall pluck your feet out of the net."

Psa. xxv. 15.

"Jesus, my strength, my hope,
 On Thee I cast my care,"
(my spiritual care,)
"With humble confidence look up.
 And know Thou hear'st my prayer.

"Give me on Thee to wait
 Till I can all things do,
On Thee Almighty to create,
 Almighty to renew."

VI.

THE DIVINE FRIEND.

"THE Lord as Friend" is our present topic. Our two previous chapters stand in close connexion with this. We saw that the Lord as Keeper was an idea in deepest union with that of the Lord as Master. So now with this other. The divine Friendship of Christ Jesus is a thing revealed to the soul which He owns, the soul which He keeps. He who would know Him as Friend, in all the depth and reality of the blessed character, must be he who has put his neck beneath the Master's yoke, and committed himself into the Possessor's custody; that blissful captivity, that *custodia militaris*, as a

Roman might have called it, in which the soul recognizes that it is ever the prisoner of the Lord, and rejoices to know not only that He has clasped its hand in love with a clasp that is returned, but that the two hands are chained together with the strong bond of a real, a lawful, an absolute, an acknowledged, conquest and custody.

Happy we, if we are learning what it is to move about day by day, in thought, word, and act, alone, or in the circle, or in the throng, conscious that we are thus attached to the never-sleeping Keeper of the soul; really bound, and not wishing to be free.

But now, not for a moment leaving these facts behind, taking them with us, weaving them into all that is to follow, we pass on to the view of the Divine Friend.

Remember then, first, the assurances in

the Word of God of the fact that such the Lord is. "I say unto you My friends"; "I call you not slaves, I call you friends." And, in less direct but profoundly significant phrases, "I will come unto him, and make My abode with him"; "I will sup with him, and he with Me"; "I will manifest Myself to him"; "Our fellowship," our share of thought, and view, and sympathy, "is with the Father and with His Son, Jesus Christ." _{Luke xii. 4. Joh. xv. 15. Joh. xiv. 21, 23. Rev. iii. 20. 1 Joh. i. 3.}

Remember again what these and the like Scriptures imply in the idea of the friendship of the Lord. It is an idea, not merely of patronage and benevolence on His part, as when a Christian philanthropist is said to be the friend, the best friend, of the outcast, the falling, or the fallen. It is that of intimacy, of reciprocity, of holy interchange of thought and feeling. "I will sup *with him*," as

well as, "he with Me"; "We have fellowship one with another"; "The slave knoweth not what his lord doeth; but all things that I have heard of My Father I have made known to you."

Rev. iii. 20.
1 Joh. i. 7.
Joh. xv. 15.

And how closely the Lord connects this with the obedience of the faithful soul! "Ye are My friends, if ye do whatsoever I command you"; "He that hath My commandments, and keepeth them, he it is that loveth Me, and I will love him, and will manifest Myself to him"; "If a man love Me, he will keep My words; and My Father will love him, and We will come unto him, and make Our abode with him."

Joh. xv. 14.
Joh. xiv. 21, 23.

And this reminds us, if we need it, of the special character of this wonderful mutual intimacy. It is the friendship of truly sympathetic persons; capable, marvellously capable, of mutual intuitions and responses of thought and will. But

then it is a case where always, and in deepest realization, one is subject, the other King; one is slave, the other Master For we said above (p. 47), that when the Lord says, "I call you not slaves," the absolute words have a relative bearing. In the very same conversation He says, "Ye call me Lord, and ye do well, for so I am." He prompts His loved ones to glory in the life-long title, "slave of Jesus Christ." He claims the entire disposal of their lives: "What is that to thee? follow thou Me." Nevertheless, I call you not slaves, in the hard sense of mere slavery. You are slave-friends, friend-slaves. Your *position* is unaltered and unalterable, but your *attitude* in it is divinely and blissfully modified thus, that in the depths of your recognition that you are my property, bought with a price and branded with my stigma, you are entitled, welcomed, to look into your worshipped

Master's face with eyes of true intuition into His heart, into His will, into Himself; and to welcome back, undazzled, His deep fraternal gaze into your inmost being. In the very act of claiming and taking your all in self-surrender, and of telling you all day long what to do as His conscious implements, He assures you that He knows your souls, never for a moment forgets your innermost emotions, understands you with a boundless sympathy, loves you with an indescribable affection, is not ashamed to call you brethren, tells the confessed and proclaimed slave that he is not such, but a friend.

Such is the self-surrendered believer's attitude towards the Lord, such the Lord's towards him. Profoundest reverence will look full into the eyes of unalterable sovereignty. But the gaze will be the gaze of friendship, of common understanding, of heart-embracing fellow-feeling, none the less. They have fellowship one with another.

But now what will be the spiritual effect of such a friendship on the inferior, when the superior is my Lord Jesus Christ, " my King who saved me"? *Add* to the precious views of my intense connexion with Him, as His property, His implement, His vassal, the fact that I am His friend, and He mine; that He admits me to His mind and heart, and is pleased to enter the recesses of my own, not only as the Autocrat, which He is, but as the infinitely perfect Friend. He claims to own me and to use me as despotically as if I were inanimate; and let me remember this always, let me remember it now. But He comes down into my soul with the large and loving assurance that He sees in me all the while His conscious friend, and gives Himself to me for mine. He invites me to the utmost confidence I care to place in Him. He requests, yes, He requests, admission into the deepest of my own. I enter His presence-chamber ere I go out to my work in His field, or when I return from it; or I look up in the midst of it, and see standing by me the Lord; and He invites me not only to clasp His feet, but to grasp His hand; nay, in the hour of need, whensoever I will, to lean upon my Master, to lay my head upon His shoulder, to tell Him all. He lets me know that He knows my sorrows. He reminds me that before I was, He is; that in my remotest memories, unutterably precious and tender, He was present, and still knows them all; that in my present toil, while in His blessed despotism He allots the task, He also perfectly understands every experience of the worker in it, and can meet them all with His sufficient grace. And in the hour of temptation it is to Him that I can confide literally *everything*—the least thing, the greatest, the worst. The insight of any other eye into my soul's recesses soon reaches its limit; the insight of His eye goes through the centre of my being, and He reserves it to Himself to deal with that. Am I conscious of failure, then? I come to Him direct, and without a moment's delay. I show Him my weakest point at its weak moment without a veil. Wonderful to say, He can make me strongest just there.

This is to put Jesus Christ's friendship to the proof; this is to find Him closer than a brother.

And if He is this to me, I shall care often to be alone with Him; and when alone, to speak with Him. It has been well said, " If you walk with God, you must talk with God, or you will soon cease to walk with God." But let not the intercourse be one-sided. Listen as well as pray. "He that hath an ear, let him hear."

For He on His part will let me look into His heart and His work. He will tell me of His thoughts of me long ago, even before the Universe began. He will explain to me the plan and way by which He made me actually His own, His property, His instrument. He will talk freely to me about the yoke, and the cross, and the thorn, as well as bid me bear them; explaining, opening up, with a friend's generous confidence, what their bearing is upon my eternal future life with Him and for Him. He will lead me out far beyond myself in His gracious expositions of His thoughts. He will talk to me about His Father, and His Father's covenant, and His Father's kingdom; about His Father's love for the world, and His Father's love for the Son, and for the Bride of His Son.

I work on the while. I submit myself with deepening simplicity to my Master. I am more than ever content to do all day long what I am told. For the bonds of absolute obligation become, in this wonderful reality of a daily intercourse, 'conductors of the living power of an eternal friendship. I would not for a moment be free, an independent agent, choosing work and bargaining for pay. I have no rights; I make no conditions. I am a "chattel that lives." But, ah! with it, and in it, and through it, I am my Master's friend; the more consciously and delightfully such, the more I own myself, first and always, His property and His slave.

> "One there is above all others
>   Well deserves the name of friend;
> His is love beyond a brother's,
>   Costly, free, and knows no end:
> They who once His kindness prove
> Find it everlasting love."

Heavenly Master, I am Thine, and Thou art mine. Show me evermore Thy heart of love, the secret of the Lord. Let nothing ever overcast this sacred friendship, to which Thou hast called me. Everywhere, always, keep me abiding in Thy love; according to the working whereby Thou art able to subdue all things to Thyself. Amen.

VII.

CHRIST DWELLING IN THE HEART.

That He would grant you to be strengthened with might by His Spirit in the inner man; that Christ may dwell in your heart by faith.—Eph. iii. 16, 17.

"CHRIST dwelling in the heart": what is the special bearing of this deep phrase, as indicated by the surrounding words?

Is it just a large re-statement of the mighty truth that "Jesus Christ is in you, except ye be reprobates"; that, in the sense of the Mystical Union, He is in us and we in Him, as the tree is in the branch, its cause of life, as well as the branch in the tree, its living effect? This is, indeed, an infinitely precious fact. It needs to enter far more than it often

[2Cor xiii. 5]

does into the daily food of the believer's spirit. True, it is a thing which ultimately passes all understanding, all analysis, so that it is soon best to pause and say, as Hooker says in another connexion, "O my Lord, Thou art true; O my soul, thou art happy." United to Him in regeneration, in re-creation, I have from Him, in no figure of speech, life, life eternal, in all the meaning of that astonishing phrase. I "have the Son," and He is my life. From Him to me flows the Virtue which is so widely different from the mere finite forces of myself. For peace, and strength, and purity, I draw upon, I drink into, that Source unfathomable, "the unsearchable riches of Christ," Who is now, even now, realized or not, in me, and I in Him. I am "joined unto the Lord"; He and I are "one spirit." Has this marvellous union been, indeed, effected?

Margin references: 1 Joh. v. 12. — Eph iii. 8. — 1 Cor. vi. 17.

Christ dwelling in the Heart.

Then let me use it; let me reckon on it in every need. In temptation, in spiritual languor and decline, in care and perplexity and toil, let me draw upon the fact—not the feeling but the fact—of "Christ in me."

The mystical union, doubtless, underlies the passage before us. But yet it scarcely forms its special teaching. For St. Paul is writing to those who undoubtedly "had the Son." And for them he prays for a new beginning, a new development; that Christ may "take up His abode" (so literally) "in their hearts by faith." For one thing, then, this surely means the warm personal realization of this mighty positive fact which we have just recalled, this vital union of the Lord with the regenerate. It means the deep reception into the inmost *heart* of the certainty that Jesus Christ is in the believer, after that indescribable but real manner.

But it means other things besides this. It means the divine reality of the *love* of the new heart to this great and blessed Christ; no mere emotional tenderness towards a humanitarian aspect of the name Jesus, but, observe, towards the "Christ," the King Messiah, the anointed One of God. It means the ocean-tide of the regenerate affections heaving towards Him. It means—what the context seems specially to indicate—an intuition, a direct gaze, into the love of Christ which passeth knowledge, into the personal application of that love; "Who loved *me*."

But is even this all? I think not. Observe the phrase, "that you may be strengthened with might by His Spirit." Here is a something, then, that needs not illumination only, nor explanation, nor invitation, but *strengthening with might*, if Christ is thus to enter in. What does this imply? That this indwelling is a thing from which the heart without such strengthening shrinks; beneath the holy weight of which it would falter and succumb. As in other things, so in this, the Spirit must "help our infirmities"; Rom. viii. 26. and here I see the truth that in this dwelling of Christ in the heart there is involved that self-surrender which without the Spirit's grace is unwelcome, impossible, but which the Spirit makes to be a thankful opening of the doors in peace to the infinitely worthy and welcome presence of the King. For if Christ inhabits the heart, it must be not only to console, but to take power and reign. And it needs a divine force beneath our will to make us, without reserve and with open eyes, assent to this and welcome Him in.

These things, at least, I read in this wonderful phrase, and they all bear upon Christian holiness. Realization of eternal

88 Christ dwelling in the Heart.

life in the Lord is here. Spiritual love to the holy Christ—love, the idea with which the context glows—is there; love continually re-generated as faith lays hold on truth and promise. And the solemn peace of self-surrender is there, the opening of the heart's door to One who must be Master where He dwells.

Touching upon another point, we briefly notice the Greek original* of the word "dwell." It denotes permanent, settled residence. "Why should He be as a wayfaring man that turneth aside for the night"? He is to be at home. The experience is to be, not intermittent, but equable; and this passage, infallible with the voice of Almighty God, is warrant that it may be. Realization of spiritual fact, the sense of spiritual love, spiritual self-surrender, may be for us, beginning now, permanent realities.

Jer. xiv. 8

* Κατοικῆσαι.

Christ dwelling in the Heart.

Then note the tense of the Greek verb. It is the aorist, and this marks a point, a crisis, a step. Not necessarily a solitary point or crisis in the history of the soul. The idea rather is of point and crisis in the abstract, realized it may be in many steps of consciousness, many upward growths and openings, a climbing ladder. Each step will be an advance so true as to be expressed in terms of a new beginning, a new entrance of the really ever-present Lord. The thought points to blissful facts of holy experience, definitely deepening views of the King in His beauty, and definite development of that likeness to Him which comes of "seeing Him as He is." _{1 Joh. iii. 2.}

Deep indeed is this one brief word of God. How much remains beyond analysis and explanation! Let us leave the subject thus, or rather let us take it up here, each for himself, in the immediate presence of Christ. With Him all thoughts of the way of holiness must begin and end. Well said the Scottish saint, Robert McCheyne, one who lived in the inner sanctuary,

> "Christ for us is all our righteousness before a holy God;
> Christ in us is all our strength in an unholy world."

VIII.

MOTIVES AND MEANS.

A FEW words shall be given to a subject which sometimes brings with it perplexity and mistake. What is the true place, in the life "lived by faith in the Son of God," for motives, for means, for helps? If it is indeed "not I, but Christ who liveth in me," what have external aids, supplies, and impulses to do for me? Have I anything to do but to yield myself, in the deep stillness of an exalted mysticism, to the play and development of that life within me which is not myself after all?

Is it so, that I am to be, more diligently

than ever, a student of written pages, a suppliant at a Throne of Grace which is quite external to me, and a plain, humble dependant on the finished work of a guilt-bearing Cross erected ages ago at a city gate far off; not on a visioned "inward cross" on which, so to speak, an atonement is wrought out in me, but on the Tree of Life and Death at Golgotha? Am I to use the fulcrums of motive? Am I to tread the ladder of a patient use of means? Let us endeavour to give some outline of an answer.

The two great factors, surely, in the walk of Christian sanctity are, on this side, self-surrender, on that side the personal power and influence of the Lord Jesus Christ in His vital, spiritual union with His servant and brother whom He has redeemed and saved. Self-surrender, in one of its brightest and truest aspects, is just the unreserved acceptance, without an *arrière pensée*, without a misgiving, of this sacred and powerful Personal Influence. And it is well, delightfully well, that the soul should habituate itself to the simplest possible attitude, as its prevailing consciousness, towards this infinitely real and blessed Person. It is well, divinely well, that in our permanently maintained "submission wholly to His holy will and pleasure," to the "ordering of all our doings by His governance," we should think and act in the main with absolute plainness and directness; going as straight as it is possible to conceive, as a matter of consciousness, to Jesus Christ, and thinking as simply as possible just this—It is Jesus Christ who lives for me and in me. It is not well, for it surely will not *work*, that every such act and thought should demand a separate analysis of reasons why, and a separate use of means.

I am under the powerful influence

of some dear and admirable earthly friend. I thankfully feel and own the impulses he gives my thought and will; the strength of his sympathy, the justness of his counsel. I know, if I stop to think, that these things are what they are to me because he is what he his; and I know, if I stop to think, that certain simple conditions are needful if I would put myself beneath their power and feel their good. But, then, I am not *always* stopping to think this. He has become to me a reality which does not need perpetual analysis. It is just he; and I go to him, and come away strong where I was weak, and happy where I was sad, and pure in purpose where I was wavering. Yet, on the other hand, I am sure to feed and develop this delightful average of habit by some definite stoppings here and there to think; by earnest memory of his conduct in the past, by deliberately watching him in the present, by taking pains to ascertain his mind and will if he has expressed it for me in writing, by freely asking him to put out more and more of his personal power upon me, and by the active meeting of his known wishes. Such things will not disturb, but, as I said, enrich and deepen the happy average, the delightful rule and habit, of personal and simple intercourse with him.

So with the soul and the Lord Jesus Christ. Continual and direct *going to Him,* or let us call it *rest upon Him,* is to be the blessed average, rule, and habit; not a fitful and intermitted thing, a glimpse of sunshine through the ponderous clouds of a winter day, but a steady "light to shine upon the road"; a "dwelling in the secret place" of the Lord. We are to ask, and to expect, that His peace shall *habitually* keep our heart

Psal. xci. 1.

and thoughts, in Him. And we are, for our inner rest and outward work alike, to think as directly and simply as possible, while we deny self and accept the daily cross, that He does the work and not we. Can we lie too simply in His hand, as our place of life and peace? Can we be too thoroughly habituated to the attitude of simply knowing, It is the Lord; I am His; He is mine? I think not. If phrases like these are not conventional but living things, they represent, I believe, just that very element which is needed to transform many a life from a course, may I call it, of earnest friction into one of power and peace, in which the Lord is "served with a quiet mind."*

But, then, this does not mean that we must never stop and think. Far from it. If those blissful formulas of life *are* to be

* Collect for the Twenty-first Sunday after Trinity.

living things and not to become, in their turn, conventions full of death, we shall do well, not always, but sometimes, often, to stop and think. "Who is He, that I should believe on Him? What has He done to me and for me, that I should live because of Him? What has He said about His personal action on me, and its modes and its measures? What does that mean—I am His? What does that mean—He is mine?" Such stoppings for thought, if made in His presence, what will they do? They will not disturb, they will enrich and develop and profoundly confirm the sweet and noble simplicity of the believer's spiritual contact with the Lord Jesus Christ as his Sanctification.

Such is some suggestion of the true place of motives and means. Let me briefly indicate further, a little in detail.

1. *Motives.*—The Word of God is

full of the appeal to motives, in the believer's walk with God. "Ye are bought with a price; therefore glorify God" (1 Cor. vi. 20); "Ye were redeemed with the precious blood of Christ" (1 Pet. i. 19); "I beseech you by the mercies of God" (Rom. xii. 1); "He was in all points tempted; let us *therefore* come boldly to the throne of grace." (Heb iv. 15, 16.) Perhaps as pregnant a place as any is Gal. ii. 20, where the great Apostle of Justification discloses to us the glorious secret of his present life of Sanctification; "not I, but Christ liveth in me"; "I live my life in the flesh by faith in the Son of God"; words impossible to take too absolutely in their blissful reality. May God the Holy Ghost make them for every true disciple the photograph of his own conscious blessedness! But do not forget how the strain closes:—"Who loved me, and gave Himself for me." Here is motive, not drawn out in argument indeed, but embosomed in living realization. I am living absolutely upon Him; I am drawing direct from His fulness; but what has brought me into contact, what enriches and develops my faith, why is Christ *in* me all this *to* me? It is because He was all that *for* me, and *towards* me.

One practical result of this view of the place of motives is, that watchful and Scriptural *meaitation* must be a very real thing with him who would live by faith in the Son, who would be "purified in heart by faith." I mean not artificial and mechanical meditation, but that direct "consideration of our Apostle and High Priest," in the light of the Written Word, of which the Epistle to the Hebrews speaks. Let our prayers not fail to have this always as a large element in them— holy contemplation, holy, humble, definite, undoubting avowal before the Lord of

Acts xv. 9.

Heb. iii. 1.

what He is, what He has done, what He is doing, for me and to me. And (here is our point) let this be with the object never to terminate the meditation, the ascription, in itself, but to contribute, as it were, just that item of fresh realization to the holy average and habit, the inarticulate consciousness, so to speak, of the soul's hourly life in and upon Him and His resources for deliverance from sin and ability to walk and to please Him.

2. But I have thus already touched on my second word, *Means*. For meditation is indeed a means, one of the innumerable means of grace. I do not attempt to speak fully of any of those means, even the chief. It will be enough if one may but emphasize the two words *means* and *grace* apart. Of grace, what shall I say? I will dare to say just this, that on the whole, and for the subject we have in hand, it is, in effect, just the

working of the Eternal Spirit, the Third Person, who evermore, as the immediate, the literally immediate, Agent, "sanctifieth the elect people of God."* And by whatever doors of inner act, or outward ordinance, He evermore comes in to do His work—with an entrance which is also residence—that is means of grace. Once for all in these chapters let me reverently do HIM His sacred honour, remembering, all through the subject, *His* work. It is He who mediates, ministers, makes, the Presence of the slain and glorified Saviour to and in the soul. "If I depart, I will send Him"; "He shall glorify me"; "I will come unto you." But this is just one of those divine truths which are meant not to encumber but to intensify the soul's personal and absolutely simple life by faith in the Son of God. Stop and think of

Joh. xvi. 7, 14; xiv. 18.

* The Church Catechism.

it, in the reverent study of the Word, and it will enhance your view of the greatness of the process that is going on; but so as to leave you the more free to act upon that process, to use to the uttermost that contact with Christ which is secured and made divinely virtual and powerful, by none other than the Holy Spirit.

Then, remembering Him, use the means by which He loves to do His spiritual work.

"Pray in the Holy Ghost." Remember that a close walk with God, by faith in His Son, is perfectly sure, if really close, to be a life of watching and prayer such as never was before; a life in which the very sense of holy joy and possession will instinctively work in you the blessed sensitiveness which must ever *ask*, while yet you *have* and *rest*.

"Search the Scriptures." For there the Spirit speaketh expressly. The closer the walk with God, by faith in His Son, the stronger will be the holy appetite for the positive assurances of your inheritance, and the positive precepts of His now delightful will, in His absolutely truthful and authoritative Word.

"WORSHIP GOD in the Spirit." Dream not that the life of faith can be its true self in neglect of the holy adorations and praises and confessions of the Lord's congregation. Expect rather to find in every public prayer of our blessed Liturgy light, truth, and help tenfold.

"Continue in the BREAKING OF BREAD." It is your LORD'S ORDINANCE, and therefore divine. At that Sacred Table, taught by the Spirit, what less do you do than put your finger into the print of the nails, and thrust your hand into His side, and say—as if indeed you saw HIM, the slain and risen Lamb—" My Lord, and my God"? Deep is the blessedness of the Communion-hour, when we are habitually living by faith in Him; a blessedness sure to enrich with new spiritual realization the daily and hourly contact with the living Lord Jesus Christ.

But there is just our point. To do *that* is the true place and work of means; to deepen, to amplify, to bind, the spiritual contact of the soul with the spiritually ever present Lord, moment by moment, day by day; the continuous "not I, but Christ," in real life; not I, but Christ in me, who loved me and gave Himself for me.

Yes, let us remember it well. Our strength against temptation, our ability for true obedience, resides in nothing less, nothing else, than living union and contact with Jesus Christ our Head. That union and contact is immediate, spiritual. NOTHING is to be between; not the most venerable and apostolic organization, not the most precious of Christ-given ordinances. But these things are not therefore nothing. Rightly used, by the spiritually-minded disciple, they have a sacred work to do. They are to be powerful things in the way of assuring the fact of contact, and of promoting, deepening, enriching, guiding, the sense of it. But the contact, the union, found and realized, is the vital thing, unique, immediate, wholly spiritual.

Will the reader make perfectly sure that THIS is the possession of his own soul? For nothing less than this is spiritual safety. Nothing else than this can bring spiritual satisfaction. It is in fact the deep secret, the substance and the sum, of CHRISTIAN SANCTITY.

IX.

SOME PRACTICAL INFERENCES.

THE earnest reader, who has followed me thus far with substantial sympathy of conviction, will bear with me in the attempt to touch, if only at a point or two, the great field of practical inference from the principles and the secret of Christian Sanctity.

We have seen that this sacred Thing is no intangible and always eluding vision. It is a reality, a fact, attainable and solid, able to be touched and clasped by the hand of faith, which itself is held within the almighty hand of the Master, Keeper, and Friend of the soul.

It is, then, a thing meant for practical

and prosaic application. It is meant to be a *phenomenon,* a thing visible, observable; not, of course, in its essence and principle, nor wholly in its results, for many of these, and the most vital of them, will take place within the world of " the inner man," witnessed only by conscience, and by the Lord, and perhaps by unseen spiritual beings. But in a thousand ways, nevertheless, Christian Sanctity will come out clear and legible to human eyes on the open page of daily life.

"Not I, but Christ," is a fact meant to shine out. It is designed, calculated, to light up the common daily path of the person whose will has really let it in. Have you said that Self, and all Self's interests and aims, are now laid at, laid under, the Master's feet? That you are literally, and wholly, not your own, but His? Then the spring and centre of your life being transferred to the will of

Another, there will be a quiet but real revolution in the working. Things will, in some very practical sense, *look* different for the change. The life lived to Self, and the life lived to the Lord, though they may often coincide here and there in details, cannot, on the whole, *look* alike.

Here let us search ourselves; or rather, let us come with the Psalmist and say, "Search me, O God, and lead me in the way everlasting." He can both search and lead. He can show us the wrong, the deflection, the inconsistency, and He can "work in us to will" the putting away, *at all costs*, whatever in our practice really contradicts the high avowal that we are HIS.

<small>Psal. cxxxix. 23, 24.</small>

How is it, then, with your TIME? You have sung, and from the heart, "Take my moments and my days." Are you "watching unto" this prayer? Do you really fill the hours, the flying hours, with the Master's business, and not at all with your own pleasure *as an end apart from Him?* He may, doubtless, make His business and your comforts to coincide. But He may not, and very often He will not, and He has the right, the full right, *never* to do so. Are you simply waiting and watching His orders what to do with this great talent of Time, ever dwindling as to quantity, ever growing in indestructible results and responsibility?

How is it with your RECREATIONS? Is His despotic will simply, and without wavering, your rule? Here are delicate problems, I know. Bodies and minds, worn and tired in this our humiliation-state, need, often need, *recreation*. And remember, the Master can enter into that need. He has not forgotten His rest by the well of Sychar, and on the cushion of the fishing-boat, and amidst the family of Bethany. But are you loyally, and in the spirit of His bondservant, consulting HIM about it all? Are you willing to yield to Him, with a smile of entire consent, your dearest earthly pursuit, if He asks for it? He may not ask you to renounce it wholly. If it consists in the exercise of special gifts of His to you, He very probably will not do so; though He may. But if He says, "Keep it, do it," He will put a new impress, a new *cachet*, upon it. Somehow or other, it will be " signed with the Cross." Literature, Music, Art of other sorts, facu'ty of speech, charm of conversation, richness of affections, wealth of knowledge, strength and skill of hand and frame, will be definitely and (sooner or later) vis'bly transformed into " vessels for the Master's use." In these matters, or some of them, you and I once *Rom. vi. 13.* " yielded our members as instruments " to unrighteous self-pleasing. Now we "yield them" in these things, in the same way, "unto God." As to the details, ask the will of God soberly, but unreservedly, with eyes open to the Bible and to your field of service, and "He shall guide thee continually." [Isa. 1 11.]

How is it with your MEANS? Surely, on plain Scripture principles, if you have the power, (and your Lord knows if you have, and you wish to go wholly by His knowledge,) you ought to devote at least a tenth* to His distinctive work. But you must not stop there. You are to recognize, whether you have a thousand a year, or ten thousand, or whether you

---

* I earnestly press this upon the reader. A devoted clergyman, intimately known to me, whose means were limited, while his family was large, once (as he told me) resolved to retrench his numerous subscriptions, and restrict them to a tithe. To his surprise he found that they were not quite a tithe as it was, and he was actually able to enlarge them.

painfully earn a little weekly, that it all belongs to Him, on the principle of divine bondservice. Your accounts must be kept for His inspection. Your casual spendings must be done as in His presence. You are to be at once thrifty and generous, because you are His trustee and His agent. In your own person you are to do your utmost to negative the reproach against the Church of Christ that a man may be converted, and yet keep an unconverted purse.

And has He given you, not money only, but wealth of other sorts? Wealth of leisure, wealth of garden, and field, and carriage, and sweet chambers of a beautiful home? Shall it be said that your use of them is precisely that of your wealthy neighbour, who honestly avows that he makes his own comfort, and this life, his aim? Ah! is it not so too often? But shall it be so now, now that you so deeply realize yourself the slave of Jesus Christ, trusted with these items of His property? No; you will find out delightful ways how to utilize them for your beloved Master. Possessions, influence, all, shall be used to bring revenue to Him. You will do good with these things, watching and loving the opportunity. The weary and the sad shall be the better for them. The poor and pleasureless shall get some gladness out of them. The household of faith shall feel a common property in them.

True, you see in His word the steady recognition of a great right of personal property. No enforced communism finds place there. But the communism of a soul that has found itself to be not its own glows from every page of Scripture; a law for Philemon who retains his household as much as for Barnabas who sells his fields.

The poorest saint may act upon it. I heard lately of one, straitened in means, but not in love, who had apportioned the very fruit-trees of her garden to the aid of this and that work for Christ. What may not the rich man do?

How is it with your FAMILY? Do you recognize that they also belong to your Master? By the Hebrew law of slavery they would do so; and they do so by the law of Christ. Is your first concern, your first prayer and effort, for your children, that they should live to God, should be of use for God? True, you cannot almightily bend their wills, nor give them grace. But you can present them unreservedly and daily to One who can. And you, by His grace, can so live before them as to commend Him to them as their end and all. And you can so manage their education as to have a first regard, and not merely a second, to their establishment in the faith, and their preparedness for God's service. Is your choice wholly thus for them? Would you very far rather see them poor, and even less completely educated, while knowing and serving Christ, than see them admirably placed, and splendidly informed, and perfectly respectable, without decision for Him?

How is it with your FRIENDS? Few questions involve more difficulty in the answer when one tries to go *à priori* into detail. But then, in a true sense, you need not do so. Take the initial step of entire recognition of the Lord's ownership over you everywhere and in everything, and more and more the crooked things will be made straight. Are you doing this? Do you entirely recognize that your friendships are things to be formed and carried on under your Master's eye, and as by His slave who is also His friend? Are you entirely willing to consult Him, your inmost Friend, about the whole problem? The simplicity of the will in this matter will solve a thousand complexities of the circumstances. You will surely see, with a holy tact, how and when to be " in the world," in a social sense, while " not of it," and how and when with quiet decision to break off, to retire, to decline; how to be silent; how to speak; how always to witness for your Lord in the tone and temper of common intercourse.

With this fragment of practical thought I leave the blessed subject we have had before us, or rather let me turn, humbly and in the strength of Christ, to life, and to this hour's calls to live to Him as His own.

Our position, our secret, as His slaves, His implements, His friends, His members, we must carry into everything, into the details of all that is modern in our English world, as well as into the hours when we retire into the great past, or the eternal future. "To the Lord" must be, will be, the motto. It will govern practice in our dress, our table, the books we read, the holidays we take, the furniture we buy. And oh! how it will govern the thoughts we think, the temper we show, the words we speak!

It will pass into the texture of our life. The spiritual, by a sacred law, will descend evermore into the practical. To us "to live shall be Christ." He will be made to us, in all the experiences of human doing and being, Sanctification.

Phil. i. 21.
1 Cor. i 30.

"Christ is ALL—the love of Christ—the power of Christ. More than all in Thee I find. I have *found* more in Him then I ever expected to *want.*"

Life of the Rev. T. SCOTT, p. 378.

HYMNS.

"Yield yourselves."—ROM. VI. 13

My glorious Victor, Prince divine,
Clasp these surrender'd hands in Thine
At length my will is all Thine own,
Glad vassal of a Saviour's throne.

My Master, lead me to Thy door;
Pierce this now willing ear once more:
Thy bonds are freedom; let me stay
With Thee, to toil, endure, obey.

Yes, ear and hand, and thought and will,
Use all in Thy dear slavery still!
Self's weary liberties I cast
Beneath Thy feet; there keep them fast.

Tread them still down; and then, I know,
These hands shall with Thy gifts o'erflow,
And piercèd ears shall hear the tone
Which tells me Thou and I are one.

H. C G. M.

March. 1885.

"I will give you rest."—MATT. XI. 28.

My Saviour, Thou hast offer'd rest,
   Oh, give it then to me;
The rest of ceasing from myself,
   To find my all in Thee.

This cruel self, oh, how it strives
   And works within my breast,
To come between Thee and my soul,
   And keep me back from rest.

How many subtle forms it takes
   Of seeming verity,
As if it were not safe to rest,
   And venture all on Thee.

And yet it was no little price
   That bought this rest for me;
'Twas purchased at the mighty cost
   Of Jesu's agony.

I only enter on the rest
  Obtain'd by labours done;
I only claim the victory
  By Him so dearly won.

And, Lord, I seek a holy rest,
  A victory over sin;
I seek that Thou alone shouldst reign
  O'er all, without, within.

In Thy strong hand I lay me down,
  So shall the work be done;
For who can work so wondrously
  As an Almighty One?

Work on, then, Lord, till on my soul
  Eternal light shall break;
And in Thy likeness perfected,
  I, satisfied, shall wake!

E. H. H.

From *One Hundred Hymns*, by kind permission of the Publisher, Mr. J. Taylor, Edinburgh.

" Mine eyes are ever toward the Lord, for He shall pluck my feet out of the net."—PSALM XXV. 15.

A VOICE, a call from glory, cries
" Watch, Christian, watch, at eve, at morn,
Lest open violence, or surprise,
  Defeat thy soul forlorn."

My Saviour, Master, it is Thou!
Thy voice awakes me to the strife!
Yes, let me watch—each passing Now,
  Each conscious pulse of life.

Yet how can this unready will
At once, at every point, repel
The heart's own traitors, aided still
  By energies of hell?

A sinner's watch against his sin
I keep, with weary sighs, in vain;
In vain on evil deep within
  This aching gaze I strain.

But now a better hope is mine;
JESUS, 'tis Thou, my life, my own;
Bid through the Word Thy Spirit shine,
    And show THYSELF alone.

To see the glory of Thy Name,
Eternal SON for sinners given;
To embrace Thy Cross for aye the same,
    Thy Gift of peace, of Heaven;

To welcome Thy great Light at length;
Thy love unknown to trust, to know;
This brings a tenderness, a strength,
    Nought else can give below.

Then to my soul each anxious morn,
Each toiling noon, each wearied eve,
The sweet, the blissful thought be borne,
    " Thou livest—I believe."

Thus shall I learn a wakeful power
Within me felt, yet not of me;
Thus meet the foes of each new hour
    By looking unto Thee.

H. C. G. M

"He that is joined unto the Lord."—1 Cor. vi. 17.

Dear is Thy Presence with Thy friends
　To faith's glad eyes reveal'd,
Their sun when sorrow's night descends,
　In battle's hour their shield.

But oh, when inmost spirits faint,
　'Tis life to clasp the Word
That tells of Thee with every saint
　For ever One, dear Lord.

Companions may converse and go;
　But what shall now divide
Members and Head, above, below,
　The Bridegroom and the Bride?

H. C. G. M.

March, 1885.

"*This Cup is the New Covenant.*"—LUKE XX. 22.
See Heb. x. 16, 17.

BEFORE Thy Table, Lord, I kneel,
　　And clasp the Cup of holy Wine,
The great New Covenant's royal Seal,
　　Authentic, visible, divine.

Thy twofold grant, it all is here,
　　The death-bought Peace, the cleansing Power;
Sure is Thy Seal, my title clear;
　　I claim the whole this blissful hour.

　March, 1885.　　　　　　　H. C. G. M.

"*He hath clothed me with the garments of salvation.*'
—ISA. LXI. 10.

CLOTHED in Thy righteousness, wash'd from my sin,
Hearing the Spirit's voice witness within,
Lo! I before Thee bow and adore Thee,
　　Ever the same.

Shine with the light of Immanuel's face,
Infinite holiness, infinite grace;
Shine on me ever, so to be never
   Darken'd with sin.

Fain would I ever abide in Thee, Lord!
Fain with Thy presence be fill'd, and
   Thy word,
Now, now receive me, never to grieve
   Thee,
   Never to stray.

Holy, thrice Holy! Thy pardoning love
Draws me to join the blest spirits above,
Whose never-ending praises, ascending,
   Circle Thy throne!

Henry Moule

1871.

www.ingramcontent.com/pod-product-compliance
Lightning Source LLC
Chambersburg PA
CBHW020121170426
43199CB00009B/587